WHAT I LOVE ABOUT

MOM

WRITTEN BY

_____

ADDITIONAL FREE RESOURCES

Visit:
www.rocketstudiobooks.com/love

Get:
- Ideas & inspiration to make your book pop!
- A page of all the questions to draft your answers

JOIN US ON INSTAGRAM

@LotusLovePress

LOTUS LOVE PRESS

01

I LOVE IT WHEN WE

02

THANK YOU FOR TEACHING ME

_____

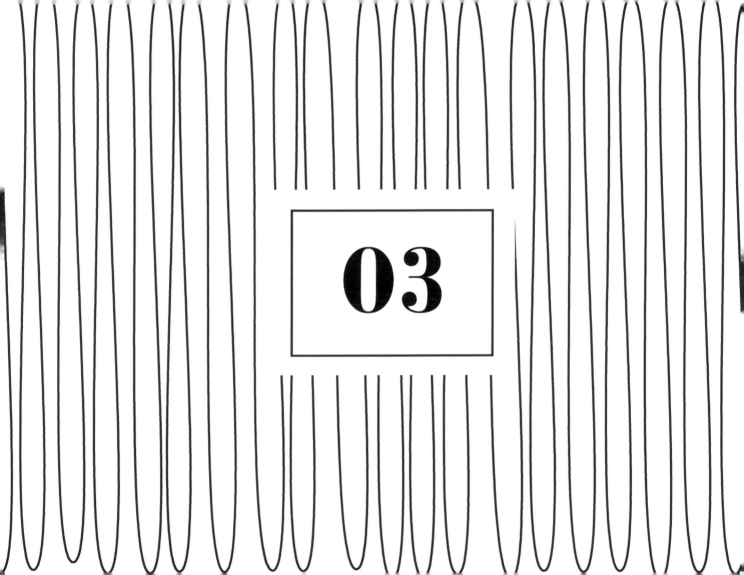

03

I KNOW YOU LOVE ME BECAUSE

_____

04

I LOVE HOW YOU ALWAYS

THANK YOU FOR

06

THE FUNNIEST THING ABOUT YOU IS

_____

YOU ARE REALLY GOOD AT

_____

08

I LOVE IT WHEN YOU SAY

_____

09

IF YOU WERE AN ANIMAL, YOU'D BE

_____

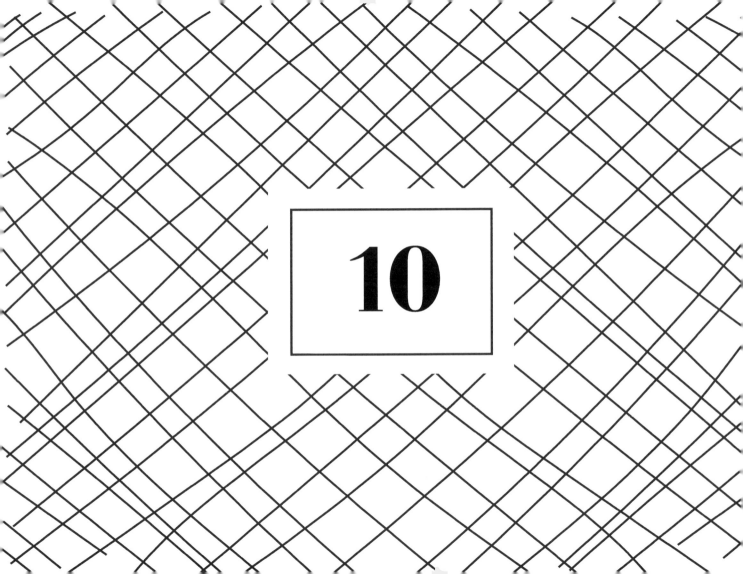

10

YOU MAKE ME LAUGH WHEN

_____

11

I'M GLAD WE

12

THE BEST THING ABOUT YOU IS

_____

13

YOU ARE BETTER THAN A

_____

YOU TAUGHT ME HOW TO

15

I LOVE HOW YOU NEVER GET TIRED OF

16

I LOVE IT WHEN WE PLAY

_____

17

IF YOU WERE A DESSERT YOU'D BE

18

WHEN YOU LOOK AT ME I FEEL

_____

19

MY FAVORITE THING WE'VE DONE WAS

_____

20

I LOVE TO WATCH YOU

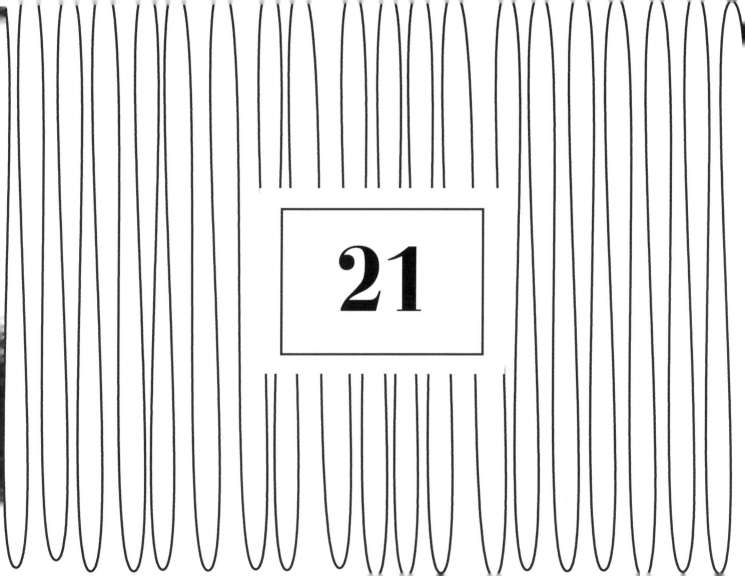

21

YOU MAKE ME WANT TO BE BETTER AT

_____

22

YOU MAKE THE BEST

_____

23

ONE WORD TO DESCRIBE YOU IS

24

IF YOU WERE A COLOR YOU'D BE

25

I LOVE THAT YOU'RE
MY MOM BECAUSE

_____

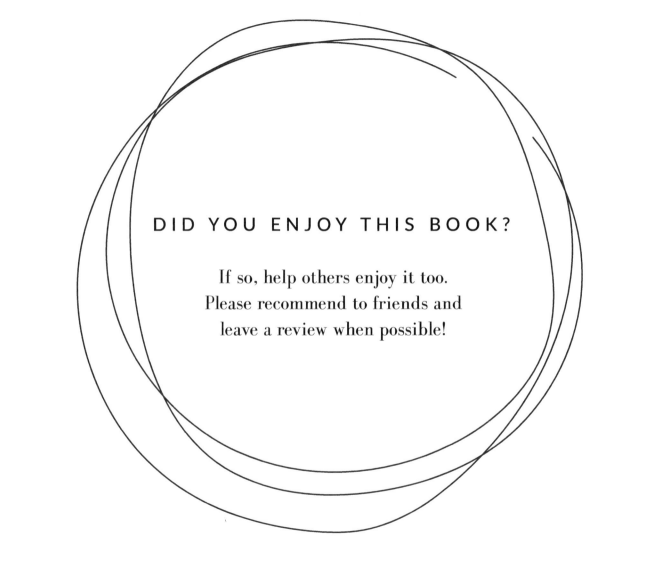

DID YOU ENJOY THIS BOOK?

If so, help others enjoy it too.
Please recommend to friends and
leave a review when possible!

THERE'S A BOOK FOR EVERYONE YOU LOVE!

Grandparents	Parents	My Daughter
Grandma	Mom	My Son
Nan	My Mommy	My Step Daughter
Nana	My Stepmom	My Step Son
Nanna	Mum	My Granddaughter
Granny	My Mummy	My Grandson
Grammy	My Stepmum	My Aunt
Gigi	Dad	My Auntie
Nonna	My Daddy	My Aunty
Mimi	My Stepdad	My Uncle
Oma	My Wife	My Nephew
Abuela	My Husband	My Niece
Grandad	My Boyfriend	
Grandpa	My Girlfriend	
Pa	My Partner	
Pop	My Sister	
Papa	My Brother	
Opa	Things I Love about You	
Nonno		

SCAN ME

FIND US ON AMAZON

LOTUS LOVE PRESS

Made in the USA
Columbia, SC
07 May 2025